PIANO • VOCAL • GUITAR

The New Complete
Wedding Songbook

This publication is not for sale in
the EC and/or Australia
or New Zealand.

Cover photo: Fred Sieb

HAL•LEONARD™
CORPORATION
7777 W. BLUEMOUND RD. P.O. BOX 13819
MILWAUKEE, WISCONSIN 53213

BRIDAL CHORUS

(From "Lohengrin")

RICHARD WAGNER

3

WEDDING MARCH

FELIX MENDELSSOHN

Majestically

THE HAWAIIAN WEDDING SONG

English Words by AL HOFFMAN & DICK MANNING
Hawaiian Words & Music by CHARLES E. KING

Slowly, with much warmth

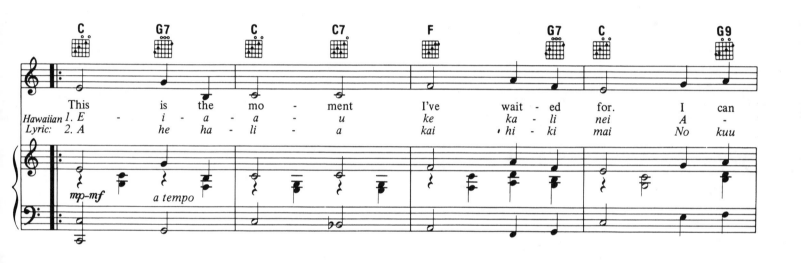

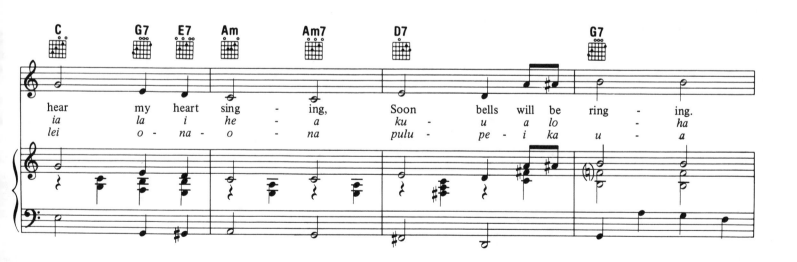

ANNIVERSARY SONG

By AL JOLSON
and SAUL CHAPLIN

CANON IN D

Johann Pachelbel
Arranged by MARION VERHAALEN

TOO MUCH HEAVEN

Words and Music by BARRY GIBB,
ROBIN GIBB and MAURICE GIBB

Slow Ballad tempo

Dmaj7 · F#m7 · Gmaj7

No-bod-y gets too much heav-en no more, it's much hard-er to come by; I'm

Dmaj7 · A7sus · Dmaj7

wait-ing in line. _____ No-bod-y gets too much

Repeat and Fade

WHEN I NEED YOU

Moderately, with feeling

Words by CAROLE BAYER SAGER
Music by ALBERT HAMMOND

I LOVE YOU TRULY

CARRIE JACOBS - BOND

AIR
(from Water Music Suite)

Slowly and stately

G. F. HANDEL

LONGER

Words and Music by
DAN FOGELBERG

Moderate Ballad

Long - er than__ there've been fish - es in the o - cean,
Strong - er than__ an - y moun - tain cath - e - dral.
Through the years__ as the fi - re starts mel - low,

YOUR SONG

Slow, but with a beat

Words and Music by ELTON JOHN and BERNIE TAUPIN

LOVE'S GROWN DEEP

Words and Music by
KENNY NOLAN

THE ANNIVERSARY WALTZ

Words and Music by
AL DUBIN and DAVE FRANKLIN

Moderately

Tell me. I may al - ways dance The An - ni - ver - sa - ry Waltz with

you._____ Tell me this is

real ro - mance, An an - ni - ver - sa - ry

dream come true._____ Let

this be the an - them to our fu - ture

ped.

JESU, JOY OF MAN'S DESIRING

By J.S. BACH

Ho - ly wis - dom,
Hark, what peace - ful

love____ most____ bright,
mu - sic____ rings,

Drawn by the
Where

Thee, our souls as - pir - ing,
flock in Thee con - fid - ing,

Soar to un - cre -
Drink of joy from

at - ed _____ light.
death - less _____ springs.

Word of God our flesh_____ that
Theirs is beau - ty's fair - est

fash - ioned,
plea - sure,

With the fire of life_____ im -
Theirs is wis - dom's ho - liest

pas - sioned.
trea - sure.

Striv - ing still to truth un -
Thou dost ev - er lead Thine

known,
own,

Soar - ing
In - the

dy - ing
love - of

round_____ Thy_____
joys_____ un -

throne.
known.

FEELINGS
(¿DIME?)

English Words and Music by MORRIS ALBERT
Spanish Lyric by THOMAS FUNDORA

Moderately Slow

THE LORD'S PRAYER

ALBERT HAY MALOTTE

I JUST FALL IN LOVE AGAIN

Words and Music by
LARRY HERBSTRITT, STEPHEN H. DORFF,
GLORIA SKLEROV and HARRY LLOYD

LOVE ME TENDER

Words and Music by
ELVIS PRESLEY & VERA MATSON

1. Love Me Ten - der, love me sweet;
2. Love Me Ten - der, love me long;
3. Love Me Ten - der, love me dear;

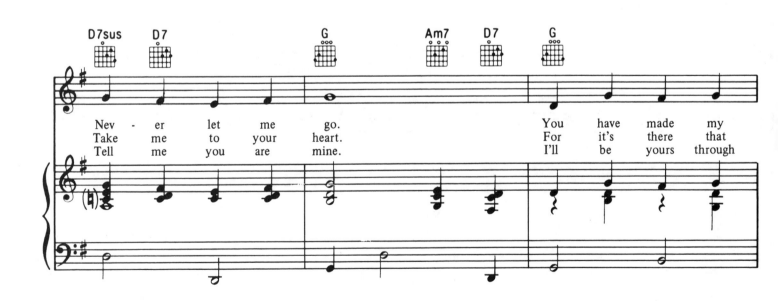

Nev - er let me go. You have made my
Take me to your heart. For it's made there that
Tell me you are mine. I'll be yours through

EXTRA VERSE   4. When at last my dreams come true,
Darling, this I know:
Happiness will follow you
Everywhere you go.

MELODY OF LOVE

Lyric by TOM GLAZER
Music by H. ENGELMANN

THROUGH THE YEARS

Words and Music by
STEVE DORFF and MARTY PANZER

TRUMPET VOLUNTARY

JEREMIAH CLARKE

WHITHER THOU GOEST

Words and Music by
GUY SINGER

HOW DEEP IS YOUR LOVE

Words and Music by BARRY GIBB,
ROBIN GIBB and MAURICE GIBB

Moderately

COULD I HAVE THIS DANCE

Words and Music by
WAYLAND HOLYFIELD
and BOB HOUSE

AVE MARIA

Very slowly

Music by FRANZ SCHUBERT
Traditional liturgical text

*pronounced grah - tsee - ah

na, A - ve, A - ve! Do - mi - nus Do - mi - nus____ te - cum, Be - ne -

di - cta tu in mu - li - e - ri-bus, et be - ne - di - ctus, et

be - ne - di - ctus fru - ctus ven - tris, ven- tris, tu - i, Je - sus.**

A - ve Ma - ri - a!

** pronounced yeh - zoos

To Coda ⊕

ho - ra mor - tis no - strae, in ho - ra mor - tis, mor - tis no - strae, in

ho - ra mor - tis no - strae. A - ve Ma - ri -

D.S. al Coda

a!

CODA

dim.

TRY TO REMEMBER

Words by TOM JONES
Music by HARVEY SCHMIDT

JUST THE WAY YOU ARE

Words and Music by
BILLY JOEL

Don't go chang-ing ___ to try and please me ___ You nev-er

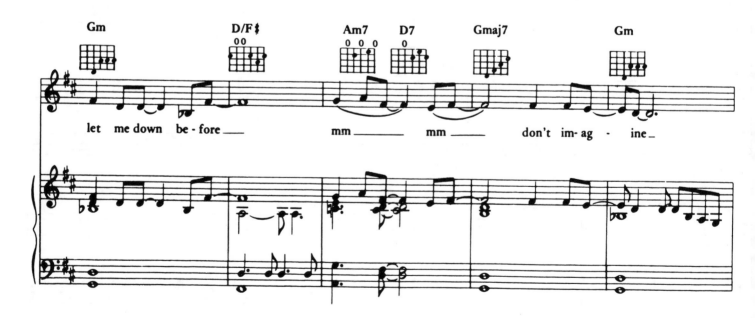

let me down be-fore ___ mm ___ mm ___ don't im-ag - ine ___

84

YOU NEEDED ME

Words and Music by
RANDY GOODRUM

Moderately

YOU'RE MY EVERYTHING

Words and Music by J.M. de SCARANO
N. SKORSKY and L. GOMEZ

ODE TO JOY

Music by LUDWIG VAN BEETHOVEN
Words adapted from FRIEDRICH SCHILLER

Moderately

LET ME CALL YOU SWEETHEART
(I'm In Love With You)

Words by BETH SLATER WHITSON
Music by LEO FRIEDMAN

ENDLESS LOVE

Words and Music by
LIONEL RICHIE

BECAUSE

Words by EDWARD TESCHEMACHER
Music by GUY D' HARDELOT

AND THIS IS MY BELOVED

(From the Broadway Production "KISMET")

Words and Music by ROBERT WRIGHT
and GEORGE FORREST

FOR ALL WE KNOW
(From the Motion Picture "LOVERS AND OTHER STRANGERS")

Words by ROBB WILSON and JAMES GRIFFI
Music by FRED KARLI

Moderato, with a light beat

Love, _____ look at the two of us, _____ Stran-

gers _____ in man- y ways. _____

IF WE ONLY HAVE LOVE

English lyrics by
MORT SHUMAN and ERIC BLAU
Original French lyrics by JACQUES BREL
Music by JACQUES BREL

TRUMPET TUNE

JEREMIAH CLARKE

Stately

WEDDING PROCESSIONAL
(From "The Sound Of Music")

Words by OSCAR HAMMERSTEIN II
Music by RICHARD RODGERS

Majestically

For the entrance of the Bride

TRUE LOVE

Moderately Slow

Words and Music by
COLE PORTER

SUNRISE, SUNSET
(From the Musical "FIDDLER ON THE ROOF")

Lyrics by SHELDON HARNICK
Music by JERRY BOCK

Moderately Slow Waltz tempo *(soulful and wistful)*

OH PROMISE ME!

Words by CLEMENT SCOTT
Music by REGINALD DE KOVEN

CAN'T HELP FALLING IN LOVE

Words and Music by
GEORGE WEISS, HUGO PERETTI,
LUIGI CREATORE